FULL-SPEED SPORTS

THE SCIENCE OF A SLAP SHOT

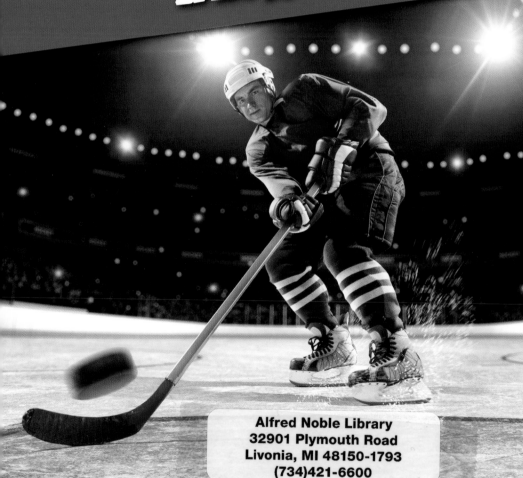

ELLEN LABRECQUE

Published in the United States of America by Cherry Lake Publishing
Ann Arbor, Michigan
www.cherrylakepublishing.com

Content Adviser: Erik Zobel, Amherst High School Physics, Amherst, New York
Reading Adviser: Marla Conn, ReadAbility, Inc.

Photo Credits: © Aksonov/iStock.com, cover, 1; © SMI/Newscom,5; © Wickedgood | Dreamstime.com - Zdeno Chara Boston Bruins Photo, 6; © Jupiterimages/Thinkstock Images, 9; © Raytags | Dreamstime.com - Hockey Stick And Puck Photo, 10; © Ivica Drusany/Shutterstock.com, 11; © IHA/Icon SMI 524/IHA/Icon SMI/Newscom, 13; © Eric Fahrner/Shutterstock.com, 15; © Modestil | Dreamstime.com - Hockey Photo, 16; © Wickedgood | Dreamstime.com - Kostitsyn Checks Patrice Bergeron (NHL Hockey) Photo, 19; © Kevin Norris/Shutterstock.com, 20; © lsantilli/Shutterstock.com, 21; © Laszlo Szirtesi/Shutterstock.com, 22; © technotr/iStock.com, 25; © Jmweb7 | Dreamstime.com - Hockey Sticks Photo, 26; © Tumar/Shutterstock.com, 28

Library of Congress Cataloging-in-Publication Data

Labrecque, Ellen.
  The science of a slap shot/Ellen Labrecque.
    pages cm.—(Full-Speed Sports)
  Includes bibliographical references and index.
  ISBN 978-1-63362-584-6 (hardcover)—ISBN 978-1-63362-764-2 (pdf)—ISBN 978-1-63362-674-4 (paperback)—ISBN 978-1-63362-854-0 (ebook)
  1. Hockey—Juvenile literature. 2. Sports sciences—Juvenile literature. I. Title.

  GV847.25.L34 2015
  796.356—dc23
                        2015005833

Cherry Lake Publishing would like to acknowledge the work of
the Partnership for 21st Century Skills. Please visit www.p21.org
for more information.

Printed in the United States of America
Corporate Graphics

ABOUT THE AUTHOR

Ellen Labrecque is a freelance writer living in Pennsylvania with her husband and two kids. She has written many non-fiction books and previously was an editor at *Sports Illustrated Kids* magazine. An avid runner, Ellen is always trying to figure out ways to become speedier.

TABLE OF CONTENTS

CHAPTER 1

Ice Hockey's Strongest Player

The score is tied 2–2 in a 2014 National Hockey League (NHL) game between the Boston Bruins and the New York Rangers. With just under nine minutes to play in the third period, Zdeno Chara of the Bruins winds up to take hockey's hardest shot, the slap shot. The slap shot is for ice hockey what a powerful swing is for baseball. A powerful slap shot can get an arena of fans on their feet, hoping for a goal.

Chara is the tallest player ever to be in the NHL. The 6-foot-9 (205.7-centimeter), 260-pound (118-kilogram)

Zdeno Chara has the fastest slap shot in the NHL.

Zdeno Chara winds up for a slap shot.

LOOK!

Look at how Chara has his legs and arms positioned. Do you think this will be a hard slap shot or just a little tap? How can you tell? Keep reading to see if you're right.

defenseman twists his upper body and reaches back with his stick. The stick lifts way up toward the rafters. As he swings, his stick moves so fast, you can barely see it. Chara transfers his weight from his back leg to his front leg and makes contact with the puck. *Whack!* The black blur goes flying toward Rangers goaltender Henrik Lundqvist at about 100 miles (161 kilometers) per hour (mph). After Chara fires his shot, he is knocked down to the ice, but the puck sails between Lundqvist's pads. *Goal!* While still on his knees, Chara pumps his fists in the air in celebration. The Bruins hold on to the lead and win, 3–2.

Chara holds the record for the hardest shot in the NHL. In 2012, during the Hardest Shot competition at All-Star Weekend, he fired the puck at 108.8 mph (175.1 kph)! This is even faster than Major League Baseball's fastest pitch record of 108.1 mph (174 kph).

How does Chara make the puck fly so fast? He follows the scientific rules behind the slap shot. Let's learn how to make the puck zoom at lightning speed!

CHAPTER 2

THE HISTORY OF THE SLAP SHOT

Ice hockey is the fastest-moving team sport. Players skate as fast as 30 mph (48 kph), and the puck flies at over 100 mph (161 kph). The first recorded indoor ice hockey game was on March 4, 1875, in Montreal, Canada. Nine players from each team took the ice, instead of six like in the modern game. They played with a wooden puck and wooden sticks. The National Hockey League was founded more than 40 years later, in 1917. The league included five teams, all from Canada.

Hockey has been popular in Canada for hundreds of years.

In the early days of ice hockey, sticks were made entirely of wood, which didn't bend or flex much. In the 1950s, manufacturers started making stick blades from plastic instead of wood. These sticks were stronger yet lighter than the wooden ones. They were also cheaper to make. Later that decade, players began to bend their stick blades before games, giving the blades a curved shape. Andy Bathgate, from the New York Rangers, is traditionally given credit for this. When a slap shot is

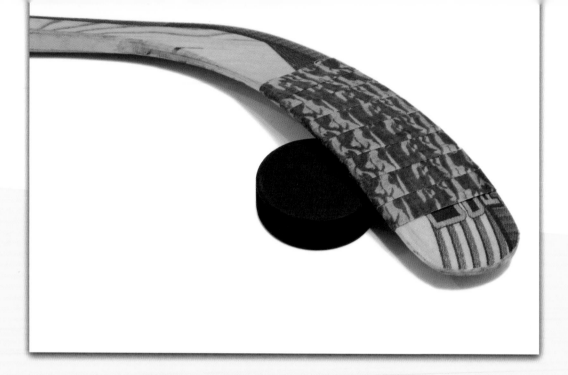

Wooden sticks, like this one, don't bend as easily as sticks made of composite material.

hit with a curved blade, the puck moves in unexpected ways. The **unpredictability** of puck movement makes it much harder for goalies to stop shots. Once stick manufacturers saw that the players were experimenting with curving their blades, they began to produce sticks this way. Modern sticks are made of a **composite material** that lets them bend or **flex** a lot.

Back when ice hockey was only played outside, some players made pucks of cow dung! The first rubber ice hockey pucks were made from rubber balls sliced in half.

Today, the NHL uses pucks made from hardened rubber. A puck is 3 inches (7.6 cm) across and 1 inch (2.5 cm) thick, and weighs about 6 ounces (170 grams), about as heavy as an apple. The NHL freezes their pucks before using them in games. Frozen pucks are less bouncy and easier to control than unfrozen ones. In an NHL game, the referees replace the puck with a newer, colder one after every couple minutes of gameplay.

Pucks need to be replaced several times per game.

Alex Shibicky of the New York Rangers is credited with inventing a version of the slap shot back in the 1930s. Now, the shot he used is considered more of a "snap shot," because he did not raise his stick higher than the knees. Still, Shibicky described his shot as moving "just like a bullet. Then, when you follow through, it's the most beautiful shot you'd ever want to see."

Fast-forward 15 years, and Bernard "Boom Boom" Geoffrion of the Montreal Canadiens is given credit for inventing the slap shot we are more familiar with today. He was the first to bring his stick far above his head

THINK ABOUT IT!

Before the 1950s, goalkeepers didn't wear masks. Now, all ice hockey goalies wear masks, as well as plenty of other padding to keep themselves safe. The thicker the padding, the more it can protect goalies against the **force** of a puck. (Imagine an airbag inflating to protect someone in a car accident.) Do you think the players should be able to choose for themselves how much safety gear to wear? What might happen if they wear too much or too little? How could this impact the game?

Jacques Plante developed an early version of a face mask for goalies.

when shooting. His nickname came from the sounds of his stick booming off the puck and then the puck booming off the boards.

Bobby Hull, of the Chicago Blackhawks, made the slap shot popular. Although technology at the time wasn't able to accurately record the speed, *Popular Mechanics* magazine estimated Hull could make the puck fly at speeds of over 100 mph (161 kph). In 1966, he became the first player to score more than 50 goals in a season. Many of these goals were the result of his fearsome slap shot.

CHAPTER 3

SUPER SLAP SHOT SCIENCE

The game of ice hockey has gotten faster, and shots have gotten fiercer, over the years. Much of this advancement is due to better technology, training, and nutrition. But the scientific principles behind the slap shot have remained constant over the years. Why? Because they work!

The slap shot actually takes longer to execute than other shots. It also requires a lot of space for the player to perform it.

Players must have room to windup for a slap shot.

When a player takes a slap shot, the first step is the windup. In the windup, the player's shoulders and upper torso act like a **fulcrum**, or turning point. The hockey stick acts as the **lever** that is turned by the fulcrum. The player rotates his upper body backward until his stick reaches way over his head. Then, as he gets ready to strike the puck, he rotates his weight from his back skate to his front skate. This weight shift helps transfer the **momentum** he gained from

A hockey stick is full of potential energy as it comes in contact with the puck.

the stick and skating movement toward the puck. This also means a bigger and taller player would generate more force than a smaller and shorter one, if done correctly.

Before the player's stick strikes the puck, the blade slightly slides along the ice. This helps the stick flex, or snap back, and loads it with **potential energy (PE)**. When the stick slides along the ice, it is like pulling back on a slingshot before shooting it. The PE the flexed stick has, combined with the energy from the player, transfers to the puck to give it **kinetic energy**. The more energy that goes in, the more energy that comes out, and the more **velocity** the puck will gain.

The final step of the slap shot is the follow-through. Players follow through by pointing the stick where they want the puck to go. If they want to shoot high, they follow through high. If they want their shot low, they follow through low. *Goal!*

THINK ABOUT IT!

The NHL restricts the amount of curve on players' sticks. The league also restricts how long the stick and the blade can be. Why is this the case? If a player's stick is longer with more curve, will it generate more power? Why or why not? Go online to find out more.

HARDER, FASTER . . . SCARIER?

Ice hockey can be a dangerous sport. After all, athletes wear sharp skates and swing long sticks at frozen pucks while skating on slick ice! Thanks to training and nutrition, athletes have also gotten bigger and stronger. This means they can **check** each other and hit the puck harder.

The good news about all this danger is that these same athletes have gotten smarter about protecting themselves. The first NHL player to wear a helmet was George Owen of the Boston Bruins. Owen had played

Andrei Kostitsyn slams Patrice Bergeron into the boards.

football in college. When he joined the NHL in 1928, he wore his leather football helmet during games.

The NHL didn't make helmets mandatory until 1979. After this date, every player who entered the league had to wear one. However, players who were already in the league were allowed to go without one if they wanted to. Today's hockey helmets have a hard outer shell with soft padding inside.

The NHL has also made it safer for fans to watch games rinkside. In 2002, the NHL put netting up

Nets above the boards protect fans from flying pucks.

[21ST CENTURY SKILLS LIBRARY]

Goalies wear helmets, leg pads, gloves, and other gear.

behind the goals and in the corners of the rink. The netting protects fans from **deflected** pucks flying off the ice.

Goalie equipment has changed the most over the years. When the slap shot started to be used more often, goaltenders needed more protection. Each goalie now wears 50 pounds (22.6 kg) of protection in every game! Wouldn't you want to be covered head to toe if you were trying to stop a puck flying at speeds of 100 mph (161 kph)? The biggest change for goalies

British goalie Stephen Murphy makes a save.

[21ST CENTURY SKILLS LIBRARY]

came when they started wearing masks in the 1960s. Today, plaster molds are made of a goalie's head. These molds help create the best helmet and mask for each player. The final product is made from a material called Kevlar. This is the same material used to make bulletproof vests.

"I don't know if I would play goalie without all this equipment," says Martin Brodeur, one of the NHL's best goalies. "If a player sent a slap shot toward me, I would only be thinking about survival, not stopping goals!"

GO DEEPER!

Read this chapter closely. What's the main difference between a "snap shot" and "slap shot"? Go online to watch videos of each. What do you notice?

CHAPTER 5

SKATING INTO THE FUTURE

Thanks to new training methods and equipment, learning to hit the slap shot at blazing speeds is easier than ever. One of the most useful modern technologies that help players improve their slap shot form is the Phantom cam. This is a high-speed camera that creates super slow-motion video clips of a player shooting.

"The high-speed camera is incredible," says Julie Chu, a forward on the United States women's ice hockey team. "We know that we are flexing the stick a bit when we take a shot, but we would never know it bends that much without this technology."

Once a player watches himself on the Phantom cam, he can change his **mechanics** to make his shot better. He can twist his body a different way or shift his weight more to increase the power into his shot. This kind of information teaches ice hockey players the small tweaks they need to make to get off a better shot.

Not every goal scored comes from a slap shot.

Players often have favorite sticks that they're the most comfortable playing with.

Even though it is still in the early stages, the NHL is also experimenting with player-tracking technology. During games, computer chips are placed in the jerseys of every player, plus on the puck. These chips record the player's speed, shot locations, and even how many miles he skates per game. All of this information is sent to a computer where the results are analyzed. These chips help players improve each and every aspect of their game. The league hopes to start widespread use of this equipment in the 2015–16 season.

One of the biggest equipment advancements for improving the slap shot is the invention of composite sticks. Composite sticks are made of a variety of materials including wood, aluminum, and plastic that combine to create more powerful and durable sticks. These sticks also have more flex in their blades. All of this results in some fast-moving pucks!

GO DEEPER!

In the 1990s, there came a new invention that wasn't for the hockey players, but for the fans. The FoxTrax puck had a computer chip inside to light up when shown on a television screen, which was supposed to make it easier for viewers to follow the action. But several commentators and journalists made fun of the glowing puck, and the NHL quit using it after a few seasons. Why do you think people complained?

Hockey fans love the game's fast pace.

Ice hockey is one of the world's roughest, fastest sports. Thanks to advances in equipment and technology, it continues to get even more physical and faster—but safer too. With each and every powerful slap shot you see in the future, you will know that science played the biggest role in its success!

TIMELINE

A TIMELINE HISTORY OF HOCKEY

1875	First indoor ice hockey game is played.
1889	First women's ice hockey game is played.
1893	The first Stanley Cup is awarded to Montreal Hockey Club.
1917	The National Hockey League is formed and consists of five teams: the Montreal Canadiens, Toronto Arenas, Ottawa Senators, Montreal Wanderers, and Quebec Bulldogs.
1920	Ice hockey makes its debut at the Summer Olympics.
1924	Ice hockey makes its debut at the Winter Olympics; the NHL expands to the United States with the founding of the Boston Bruins.
1930s	Alex Shibicky invents the slap shot.
1945	The Hockey Hall of Fame inducts its first members.
1966	Bobby Hull becomes the first player to score more than 50 goals in a season. Many of these goals were the result of his slap shot.
1980	The United States defeats the USSR in the semifinal and Finland in the final to win the Olympic gold medal. The win over the USSR is called "the miracle on ice."
1980s	Aluminum sticks are used, the first that are completely non-wooden.
1990s	Sticks made of composite materials become popular.
1998	Women play ice hockey at the Winter Olympics for the first time.
2012	Zdeno Chara of the Boston Bruins sets the NHL slap shot record with a speed of 108.8 mph (175.1 kph).

THINK ABOUT IT

Think about what you knew about the slap shot and ice hockey before reading this book. Does the slap shot seem harder or easier to do now that you know the science behind it?

In chapter 3, you learned about potential energy. In ice hockey, the potential energy is loaded in the stick when it is flexed back. Can you think of other examples of potential energy in sports like baseball or tennis?

Do you think the NHL should regulate how long and how much bend a player's stick should have? Why or why not?

Do you think ice hockey is more dangerous to play than baseball? Think about the differences in equipment. Why or why not?

LEARN MORE

FURTHER READING

Frederick, Shane. *Hockey: The Math of the Game*. North Mankato, MN: Capstone Press, 2012.

Levine, Shar, and Leslie Johnstone. *Sports Science*. New York: Sterling Publishing, 2006.

Napier, Matt. *Z is for Zamboni: A Hockey Alphabet*. Ann Arbor, MI: Sleeping Bear Press, 2003.

WEB SITES

International Ice Hockey Federation
www.iihf.com
This site has information about the worldwide governing body for ice hockey and in-line hockey.

National Hockey League
www.nhl.com
Find lots of different articles, photos, and videos on the official NHL web site.

PrintActivities: Hockey Printables
www.printactivities.com/Theme-Printables/Hockey-Printables.html
Try your hand at some hockey-related games and worksheets.

GLOSSARY

check (CHEK) to use shoulders to block the progress of another hockey player

composite material (kuhm-PAH-zit muh-TEER-ee-uhl) a substance made of materials that are stronger together than they are apart

deflected (di-FLEKT-ed) made something go in a different direction

flex (FLEKS) to bend

force (FORS) an influence that causes an object to change its speed or direction of movement

fulcrum (FUL-kruhm) the pivot point where something turns

kinetic energy (ki-NET-ik EN-ur-jee) energy associated with the movement of an object, such as a hockey puck that has been shot

lever (LEV-ur) a rigid piece that transmits force or motion when a force is applied

mechanics (muh-KAN-iks) a player's movement and technique when performing an action in sports

momentum (moh-MEN-tuhm) the property that a moving object has because of its mass and its motion

potential energy (puh-TEN-shuhl EN-ur-jee) the energy that something has because of its position or the way its parts are arranged, such as a hockey stick in a windup position ready to strike the puck

unpredictability (uhn-pri-DIK-tuh-BIL-i-tee) behavior that makes it hard to say what will happen in the future

velocity (vuh-LAH-si-tee) rate of speed in a particular direction

INDEX

[21ST CENTURY SKILLS LIBRARY]